enjoy!

♡, Nikki

PALM TREES AND POSSIBILITIES

by Nikki Van Ekeren

Cover art and layout by Matt Van Ekeren

Imprint: Independently published

For information regarding permission or distribution,
contact nikkivanekeren@gmail.com

To discover more about the author visit
nikkivanekeren.com

ISBN: 978-1-7355066-2-3

LIFE LOOKS BRIGHTER WHEN YOU TRY
TO SEE THE POSSIBILITIES.

chapter 1
palm trees and possibilities

chapter 2
finding home within

chapter 3
be the flow

chapter 4
nature creates, nurture defines

chapter 5
to continue

chapter 6
the rhythm of growth

chapter 7
take the leap

chapter one

palm trees and possibilities

01

palm trees and possibilities

what if,
just for today,
you saw endless possibilities
in front of you?

what if
you anticipated the opportunities,
rather than the roadblocks?

what if
you faced every challenge
knowing that you were
capable of success?

the magic that life
has in store for us
is waiting to be seen and unleashed.
it takes an inner reset button at times
to have the eyes
to see
and the heart to feel
this type of magic.

it takes an inner compass
to navigate through the storm
and wait for the clouds to pass.

life isn't about what happens to us,
it's about how we bounce back.
hard times will always come to an end.
good times will always reappear.
which ones will you focus on?

we get to choose.
we get to see
the palm trees and
endless possibilities.

02

that inside voice

self love
is a nuanced skill
that develops with time.
when it's real,
it sticks
and grows.
when it's based on outward appreciation,
it slides up and down.

when you feel inner love,
you do not dread
doing the inner work.
you can learn
how to celebrate
those inner victories
in the middle of any circumstance.

03

be willing to accept

the powerful invisible forces
that fuel mother earth
and allow her
to grow her masterpieces
are the same forces
that flow within our bodies.
we are living works of art.

be willing to accept
the beauty that life is giving you.
be willing to learn how to see it.

you are the
emerging sculpture
created by the
genius of nature.
your life
is the masterpiece
that your vessel
gets to experience.

accept life's great gesture.
be open to all the good around you.
you are a work of art.

04

changing it up

when you relax
and let yourself
flow with life,
amazing things happen.

this means
changing up
your usual patterns and decisions.
it involves taking a risk
and branching out.

there may be comfort
in the familiar,
but there's more to feel
than just comfort.

take that new route.
eat that new food.
jump up with joy.
change it up.

05

being one with life

as a human,
we have incredible gifts
to help in our growth.
we can observe,
integrate,
learn,
engage
and seek.

these abilities
are ours to enjoy and use.
growth is a natural part
of our human journey.
remembering to be
one with life
allows us to
exercise our beautiful gifts
while not
needing to control the outcome.

we can try,
yet we have no idea
what the results will be.
our extreme control

over initiative

ignites us,

while we accept

our lack of contorl

over outcome.

go for it.

there is no need

to hold back.

let your innate ability to grow

guide you.

be one with the life you live.

06

letting the good stuff in

when you make the decision
to see the possibilities in life,
you immediately let the good stuff in.
this shift in perception
opens everything up.
your eyes need to be able
to see the good
to allow it to enter your life.

take your time.
be in the moment.
ooze your unique essence.
allow your optimistic intentions
to show you the way.

you already know
how lucky you are to be you.
live your life exuding this.
share with others your point of view,
letting them know
that it is how one sees
that determines
how one lives.

07

let go of the past

choose
to let it go.
whether it was amazing
or painful,
let it go.

allow your eyes to see
what lies ahead of you.
your future is waiting
for you to see it
and not focus so much on your past.

it's up to you.
you can let go
with grace
remembering the lessons
and forgetting the pain.

08

just for fun

when you stop taking yourself
so seriously
and turn the lens around
to see life
with fresh eyes,
you feel the glow
within and around.
the glow
that's just there
and always has been there.

it's fresh.
it's rejuvenating.
it's nourishing.

life feels fun.
you stop planning so far ahead.
any inclination you had
toward creating inner anxiety
gently breezes away.
you see the open road ahead
and smile with excitement.

09

the open road

isn't each new day
an open road
waiting for you
to experience it?

how do you see your life?

this is how
your life emerges.
your view of who you are
creates your present self.
it is the view that others see.

see your life
as your choice
and this will become
the lens in which you see.

10

the oceanic breeze

the oceanic breeze
that seems
to come from nowhere
sends the message
that anything is possible
when you believe,
when you try,
when you choose to see possibilities.

the gentle nudge
from inside
that pushes one to try,
to keep going,
to see the good around
and to forgive yourself.

the beautiful sky
that radiates hope and joy
excites one
to not hold back,
to share your light,
to explore
and to become your true self.

the shining golden sun
that brings warmth and comfort
reminds one to never back down,
to go with the flow,
to flex and grow
and to continue in the face of adversity.

life extends a lifeline
toward us
at every moment.
it may feel like a soft breeze
or the rays of the sun,
reach out and take it.

11

creating the energy around you

it is time
to ask yourself
what type of energy
you create
around you.

when you absorb information,
how do you process it?
are you able to return
to your center
when swayed from your core?
are you able to transmute
the low energy
to the high?

sit with these questions
and answer them
truthfully.

your energy,
your intention,
and your inertia
create incalculable ripples.

your power
to transform energy
is innate.

it is time to learn
how to cultivate the skills
to create the energy around you.
one poem
does not hold all the answers.
a lifetime of sincere effort
can reveal the necessary prompts
at just the right time.

ask for help.
make the intention
to create positive energy.
watch the world
make magic
through you.

palm trees and possibilities

van ekeren

chapter two

finding home within

01

finding home within

to come home
to yourself
is a long journey.
it begins with
a choice
and can become
a way of life.

it may mean
letting go of pain
to remember your power
and purity.

it may also mean
establishing new boundaries,
shedding old habits,
connecting to your intuition,
and creating the energy you emit.

it will always mean
opening up
to the inner peace
that is always there.

find home within
over and over again.

02

the beauty that surrounds me

as i run the same errands
in the same places,
i surrender to the beauty
that this simple act beholds.
my routine trip to the grocery store
rejuvenates me
as i surrender to
my intentions.

i walk into the market
with ease and gratitude
with my list of items i need
in hand.
i gather up my food
and calmly lay them out
for the cashier.

i am not in a rush
and seem to savor this ritual.
i am discovering how special
these small acts of kindness
for myself can be.

after all,

true beauty lies

in self care

and self love.

as i bestow these virtues onto myself,

i feel beautiful.

i feel happy

in my being

and my environment.

i have the eyes to see

the beauty in this moment.

03

power comes from character

power
comes
from
character.

we're trained
to think that
we need more
to be more,
but we've got
what we need.

it's about sculpting
our insides
to reveal the essence of our character,
not piling on more and more
to hopefully acquire it.

we've watched
manipulative people
steal power.
but, how do we
flex our own
muscles of power?

it's about hearing ourselves,
hearing like minded souls
and standing up for what's right.
this is power.

true power
comes from
a developed character.
there is no shortcut
to this growth.
do not let the world fool you
into thinking
that naivety is bliss.
youth may be coveted,
but wisdom is acquired and sculpted
through years of living.
true character takes time to develop.
honor this process
and share it proudly.

04

letting go is an art

sometimes,
you have to let go of yesterday
to open up to today.

letting go
is an art.
it takes practice
and intention.
it requires one
to continue to make
the same decision
over and over again.

when you let go,
you grow.
you shed the past.
you allow the future
enough space
to guide you
to your best self.

05

to begin to

to begin to see life
as an ally,
to accept today
as a gift,
to choose to be adaptable
rather than sentimental,
to leap toward
rather than to look back,
to share your gifts
rather than hoard them,
to seek
instead of sulk,
to forge ahead
with excitement
and to love and forgive yourself
before anyone else.

06

identity

when i was a child,
i thought that adults
were efficient and correct
as to label themselves
by their occupation.
this was their adapted identity.
this was a way to distinguish oneself
from the pack.

now, that i am an adult,
i see how those around me
are searching for words
in which to describe themselves.
they are hungry
for labels.
they are eager to belong
to something.

unpack
what the word
identity
means to you.
allow your own definition
of yourself

be the one that fuels you.

words emerge from an intention.
what is your intention for your life?
let this intention
be your identity.

07

seeing with new eyes

when you choose
to see with new eyes,
the landscape of your life
emerges in vivid ways.

this vividness
will be unexpected
and calm,
yet convey the most fierce
sense of peace
that you will ever know.

quiet contentment
is more powerful
than any type of drama.
it connects you to your soul
and invigorates your mind.

a calm demeanor
gives your inner world
space.
healing requires space.
loving requires space.

seeing with new eyes
always initiates growth
and fulfillment.
be open to
its slow and steady nature
and bask in its flow.

08

owning your narrative

owning your narrative
means
choosing the words
in which you describe yourself
with care.
these words empower and infuse
your life.
these words introduce
your energy.
these words show yourself
and everyone else
who you believe you are.
these words have the ability
to sing your unique song.
these words become your story.

09

the sun soaked mountains

the beauty
of the sun soaked mountains
that bask in the distance
inspires one
to pause
and to ponder.

these mountains
absorb and reflect the light
from the sun
so brilliantly.
they radiate their beauty
as only nature can.

this type of beauty exists
without shame
without suffering
without boundaries.

can we emulate such pure beauty?
can we reflect the light
that shines on us
with such radiance?
can we learn to not dim our light

when we feel fear?

maybe such questioning
is the beginning of
trying to understand
our place in nature.
as we evolve as humans,
the sun soaked mountains
will continue to inspire
and ask us to ponder.

palm trees and possibilities

van ekeren

chapter three

be the flow

01

be the flow

when we can
actively be in the moment,
we can be one with the flow.

it is not a phenomenon
that we are separate from,
we are a part of it.

the stream of life
is the ultimate flow.
it is learning
how to cease mindless thinking
and to begin to enjoy
living, observing, acting and reacting
in real time.

02

self discipline

self discipline...

means
being okay
with short term pain
for long term growth.

means making decisions
that involve
nuanced
rational thinking.

means learning to
love yourself
and do what's right for you
before others.

means enjoying
saying no
or saying yes
because either way,
it's for your benefit.

means facing inner trauma
with patience and understanding,
even when you
desire a quick fix.

means being okay
with discomfort.

self discipline
means a lot of things,
but it truly
is self love
in action.

03

doing the work

it may not feel
like your first choice
in the moment,
but doing the work
will set you free.

what do you need to face?
what do you need to do?
what do you need to feel?

just go do it.
pat yourself on the back.
smile.
sit with this feeling of accomplishment.
have a laugh for no reason.

you are doing the work
and it feels good.

04

learning how to learn

it's about
learning how to learn.

as life continually
delivers new challenges
of varying levels of intensity,
learning how to learn
lets lessons stack up
and become wisdom in action.

merging with peace
and creating inner kindness.
takes work.

it's not about
learning how to just
"get through it"
it's about learning
how to sharpen
your mental tools,
so you can navigate
through any journey.

things may go according

to your plan
or they may not.
but, at least you're
putting yourself out there.
you're feeling movement
and flow.
you are learning
in real time.

life
wants us to enjoy
this art of learning...
learning how to adapt,
how to grow,
how to thrive in new situations,
how to speak up,
how to see,
and how to fail or succeed.

trying feels good.
trying with an attitude of gratitude
and an eagerness to learn
feels amazing.

05

don't let another's actions take away your hope

don't let another's actions
take away your hope.
hope is yours.
you can always create it
from within.

the message is timeless.
the message is the continual
takeaway and reminder.

as we remember
who we are,
our power,
our worth,
and our abilities,
no one
will be able
to take away our hope.
no one can stop us
from educating ourselves,
from improving our inner and outer abilities,
from rising up
and from

exuding joy.

hope doesn't mean
turning away from it all.
hope doesn't mean being naive.
it means facing everything
with a hunger for the truth
and a quest to think rationally.

06

self help

self help
means helping yourself.
it does not matter
who knows what you do
or who appreciates the work that you've put in.
helping yourself
begins as a one person job.

07

choosing to let the worry go

i used to worry as a method
to create the notion
that i had control over every situation.
the worry would be my companion,
my constant creation,
my own doing.

i choose to let the worry go.

now that i want to see possibilities,
opportunities,
goodness,
kindness,
compassion
and excitement
rather than see the potential worst,
i no longer need to create worries in my mind.

i will continue to make this decision.
i choose to let the worry go.
i choose to participate in my life
in real time.
i choose to be flexible and open to change.
life, i choose you.

08

your version of success

what is
success to you?
open up to it
by
defining it,
feeling it,
being one with it.

enjoy it.
you are it.

flex these mantras.
seek out
your version of success.
it is waiting for you.

09

soaking it all in

when you

allow yourself

to bask in the present moment,

your body relaxes,

your mind rests

and you begin to daydream.

it feels good.

soak it all in.

10

the golden hue

when the sun makes
her entrance every morning,
there's a moment
when the sky
radiates a golden hue.

this color is so unique
to this experience
because it is alive and pulsating.
it resonates love
and hope
and joy
so abundantly
that when one is open to it,
they can immediately share
in these beautiful feelings.

that golden hue
shines light on everything.
it awakens the life force
in all living things.
it nourishes all creatures
and evokes optimism.

this energy exchange
is available to us all.
it requires nothing from the receiver.
that golden hue
is so generously shared with us
so that we can do the same.

feeling joy
and then sharing it
is what life is all about.
it is much easier than we've been taught
to access such rich feelings.

van ekeren

chapter four

nature creates, nurture defines

01

nature creates, nurture defines

if you're not
continually working on
your character,
someone else will be.

your character
is composed of
inherited and developed traits.

the character traits
that develop
from reactions
accumulate over time.
they become the
main source of who you are.

how would you like to react?
how can you make this an action?
work on this
rather than tend to
the actions of others.

what character traits
would you like to develop?

work on these
and put them at the forefront
of your mind.

continually work
on your character.
think about who you are
and who you'd like to become.
these values will forever
infuse
your character.

02

a child's eye

when did you stop seeing
through the eyes of a child?
when did you stop
looking forward to life?

perhaps, we can begin
to look at the art of growing older
as a beautiful maturation process.
once we stop creating nostalgic stories
of how much better the past was,
we can see today with fresh eyes of gratitude.

time brings wisdom.
time transforms naive joy
into rational passion
and enlightened optimism.
time is an invitation
to become your best self
through effort and work.
time allows you to see
the fruits of your labor.

enjoy it with youthful, eager eyes
and the willingness and trust of a child.

03

looking for ways in which to be happy

just like that,
i stopped worrying
and chose to look for ways
in which to be happy.
being happy is a skill.
it takes practice
and effort.

there are so many things in life
that i cannot control.
but, i can control
how i react to life.

life, i open my heart to you.
joy, i open my mind to you.
happiness, i open up my eyes to see you.

04

it's all about how you look at life

the art of seeing is a skill.
you can develop it
with patience
and a focused effort.

making a big deal out of something,
lamenting over the past,
worrying over the same things,
and not being able to appreciate the little things
will continually
get in the way of seeing the joy
that's all around you.

it's all about how you look at life.

what do you see?
how do you see?

things change when you choose how to see them.
life is waiting for you
to decide how you'd like to see it.
continual access to joy
is at your fingertips.
seize it.

05

why not choose to see the sunny side?

the sun radiates
its glow
and warmth
even when the clouds
cover it.
the darkness in your life
will always pass.
allow it to soften
and just be a phase.

you are more than pain.
the sunny side of life
is just temporarily being covered
by clouds.
let them pass.
allow the sun
to shine in.

06

choosing to see the possibilities

when something happens
that it is not a part of your plan,
take a moment to pause
and choose to see it as a possibility.

it may feel like
a problem or an inconvenience,
but is it?

the most amazing sparks of life occur
when we are least expecting them.

our eyes may not have the skill
to see the ripple effects of moments
that may change the course of our life.

the divine design of it all
will continually leave you hopeful
when you choose to see possibilities.

07

you don't need permission

i used to think
that i needed permission
to feel a certain way
and express it.
i did not want
to upset or offend anyone.
this mindset
was the driving force
behind every decision i made.

if i was happy,
but you weren't
i'd lower my frequency
to match your level.
if i was feeling joyful
and you were feeling annoyed,
i'd agree with you
and let your emotions
be the dominant force.

this way of living
did not nourish my soul.
it did not allow
genuine relationships

to flourish.
i was continually
reacting
and recalculating
how i should express myself.
i did not want
to upset the status quo,
so i'd intentionally turn
on my intuition.
i'd survey the energy
around me
to know how i should
present myself.
i would mirror
the loudest energy,
hoping to fit in.

now that i can see clearly,
i can let this habit go.
i know
that I do not have to ask
permission
to feel,
to express,

to sing my song.
i get to be me
and i am not
going to hide
or try to fit in
any longer.

08

letting the wind take your sails

when you begin to feel sorry for yourself,
you limit how far you can soar.
when you think that someone else
is to blame for your pain,
you slowly believe that happiness
is out of your grasp.
when you retreat inward as a mode of
self protection
rather than self reflection,
you may become lost to the role of victim.

when you acknowledge your power,
your abilities,
your gifts
and your inner power,
you alert life
that you are ready.
you extend your sails
and allow the wind to take you for a ride.
you show life
that you are ready for it
the good and the bad.

letting the wind take your sails
ignites and infuses
your glow,
your drive,
and your ambition.
you will have no idea what is in store for you
because it is more brilliant than your current
mind
can imagine.

trust the wind.
you're in for the ride of your life.

09

the gift of breath

to breathe in
the fresh air
of mother earth
is the ultimate gift.
this air
cleanses the soul
and nourishes the psyche.

the crisp morning air
wakes up
one's spirit
and reminds them
to seek joy.

breathe in.
breathe out.
soak it all in.

the fresh air
of mother earth
revitalizes one's purpose.
when you focus on
the gift of breath,
you become

integrated into the present moment.

life seems so vast.
life awaits you.
life loves you.

van ekeren

.

chapter five

to continue

01

to continue

to continue
in spite of your circumstances
shapes your essence
and informs your character.
this forward momentum
strengthens your muscle
of endurance and perseverance.

moving toward the future
creates a life worth living.
looking back with
regret or nostalgia
stunts this growth.
the past is a gift,
but the present will always
outshine what has come before.

to continue
in spite of
infuses your present moment
with vitality.
this will mean
changing what once was
and what always has been.

it may feel uncomfortable
and you may wonder
if you are up for the challenge.

this is your cue
to continue.
there is truly nothing to fear
when you continue
to move,
to grow,
to shine,
to show up
and to glow.

02

you are supposed to soar

we are meant
to shine
as the stars that we are.

do not be afraid.
go shine.

your essence will guide you.
your uniqueness will nourish you.

soar to new heights
that only you imagine.
trust your inner compass
and bask in your beautiful soul.
this life is yours to enjoy.

03

bring forth what is within you

believe in yourself.
bring forth what is inside of you.

share your insides with the world.
accept the fact
that you've probably been taught
to hide the most important part
about you.
know that excavating
the courage to allow this side of you
to be seen
will set you free.

ask yourself,
"what have i been scared to share?"
sit with it.
lean into it.
allow the answer to emerge.

slowly cultivate this part of you
and learn that it is a vital tool
to your wellbeing.
conjure up the bravery
to show yourself to the world.

embrace the vulnerability
that comes along with this.
this journey
will nourish you
in new ways
and lead you to
new people.

bring forth what is within you.
do not be scared of your inner beauty.
do not hoard your gifts.
share your talents
with the right audience
and allow your being to take flight.

04

let the unhealthy habits go

so often,
we continue practicing
unhealthy habits.
it can happen
unconsciously.
we may not even know
that these habits
are not good for us,
yet we persevere.

is it a way to connect
to our ancestors?
is it a way to feel
closer to our loved ones
who passed down these habits?

it does not matter
why you have done it,
it matters when you choose to let it go.

let the unhealthy habits go.
choose today.
do not fret over yesterday.
do not feel ashamed over how long

it has taken you to get here.
you have the eyes to see now.
embrace your journey.

05

when i stopped taking myself so seriously...

i can remember
snapshots of my life
with intense precision.
these vignettes of living
used to haunt me
because my brain
tinted each memory
with self doubt and shame.
my gift of recollection
was being used against me.

how did this cycle stop?
what changed?

well,
i stopped taking myself so seriously.
i realized that many of us
can remember moments in life
with utter precision.
we can remember what we said,
how it felt
and how we reacted.

this gift of memory
is not meant to haunt us.
it is not meant to play on repeat
in the psyche
to cause self torture.

allow your memory to work for you.
begin to remember
the good times.
become your own cheerleader.
this will take work at first,
but it will set in
and become your new normal.

06

start

to start something
is an act of boldness and courage.
it shows that you
have faith in yourself
and trust the flow of life.

to start something
initiates action.
this movement empowers
positive thought
and focused energy.

to start something
releases your need for control
because you've done your part,
you started.
you have no control
over the outcome.
it will unfold as it may.

keep on starting.
allow life to share its endings with you.

07

wisdom

wisdom is acquired
through living a good life.
unplug from the world
from time to time
to remember this.

there is no secret
to true wisdom,
just patience,
observation,
camaraderie
and living.

engage with your fellow humans.
share what you've got.
do not hold back.
your participation in life
will make it good.
the wisdom you need
will always surface.

08

get comfortable with greatness

do we replay
what we're used to
because we believe
that's what we deserve?
what if we became
used to exuding and feeling greatness?

it takes a moment
to change
what you're used to.
it takes moment after moment
to change your lifestyle.
change is within your grasp.
it's within you now.

greatness
is the result of
many small decisions.
it's up to you.

to pursue greatness
does not cost anything,
nor will it tire you out.
rather it will

energize you
and soothe your deepest needs.

get comfortable with your greatness.
exude it.
expect this level of living
from yourself
and from others.

09

knowing your intention

knowing your intention
creates unshakeable inner power.
when you know
the intention
behind your words and actions,
it doesn't matter what others think.

the goal
is not to get others to like you,
the goal is to love yourself
and be proud of your words and actions.

by putting yourself first,
you will be at peace with another's reaction.
by knowing why you do or say something,
you will no longer worry
about another's interpretation.

real love starts inside.
you can only share this deep rooted love
when you love yourself first,
when you are proud of who you are
and when you're not out to get others
to like you.

10

there is no need to rush

why do we rush
this moment
to get to the
next one?
what lies in the future
that is more important
than the now?

there is no need
to rush.

let your trained mind
rest into this.
you have made it.
you are here.
this is the goal.

by fully grasping
the beauty of this moment,
you will be engaged
to take each step
toward the right place.
be here.
be there.

11

slow and steady

they say
that
slow and steady
wins the race.
but,
what if
we're not trying
to win a race
and rather
we are choosing
a way of life.

to slow down
in order to
show up
with more purpose,
more of a presence
and more pure joy.

this slowness
produces
a type of steady nature
that does not need to
act impulsively.

the world may tempt or taunt,
yet we are not triggered.

we have begun
to live
with the intention
of slow and steady.
we are going with the flow
with purpose and integrity.
we become the flow.

we are not
a part of
anyone else's race.
we are creating
our own framework
of a life worth living.

12

to persevere

your muscle of resilience
is stronger than
you can imagine.
life gives you opportunities
to flex this muscle,
to lean into the pain
and to overcome obstacles.

nothing is as bad as
your mind perceives it.
let the mind speak
but choose what you listen to.

you can persevere.
you are resilient.
your mind may disagree
with you at times,
but do not succumb.

once a challenging time is over,
you can reflect and learn.
was it fun?
probably not.
did you persevere? yes.

this is what you'll remember.
this builds self trust.
this creates the life
you know is inside of you.

palm trees and possibilities

van ekeren

chapter six

the rhythm of growth

01

the rhythm of growth

everyday is an
opportunity
to see new things
emerge from
familiar places.
everyday is a chance to learn
and to grow.

there's something to learn
from every conversation
you have.
when you affix the lens
of learning
to your lifestyle,
you will grow.

nothing is too big
or too small.
all lessons have
a ripple effect.
sink into
the rhythm of growth
and allow this force
to change you.

02

choices

as you grow older,
every choice you make
begins to define who you are.
you are creating the character
you will be known as.

you may think
that you could've done better
in certain situations,
and see yourself
as a work in progress.
this is part of the human journey.
continuing to make
the same choices
that do not fuel your best self
will slowly bend and morph
your sense of self worth.

rather than lament over
previous bad actions,
take the proper time
to make the right decisions.

life is a series of unlimited choices.

each one
will add to who you are.
continue to connect
to your highest self
and watch this version of you
manifest.

03

the long game

remember in high school
when everything felt so important?
what do you remember
from it all now?

perhaps
you remember
how you did not succumb
to the peer pressure
and stood up for yourself
or maybe it was too much
and you folded under the scrutiny.

were you equipped with
a set of values to adhere to
back then?
did you check in with yourself?

regardless
of then,
this is now.

you are in the long game.
you are here

in the present moment.

the long game
challenges and invites us
to stay focused on our values
and stick to our true character.

the long game
does not pander
to the crowd
for attention or likes.

the long game
requires self discipline and will power,
yet
it is not as hard
you'd think.

it means setting an inner structure
in which to operate from,
to create values,
to think and act accordingly,
and then to move on.

be in it for the long game.

be present.

be willing to pause before you act or react.

04

curate your language

the words we use
to describe ourselves
have energetic value.
they hold something
within them.

it is time to
own our narrative.
it is time to
choose the words
that we use when we
tell our stories.

listen to yourself speak.
are you using words
that are exciting, empowering
and emboldening?
if not,
change it up.

you've got nothing to lose.
make the intention
and watch what happens.

05

everything shall pass

you are the only you,
yet, you are one among billions of others.

it may seem as if your problems are unique to you,
but you will soon discover how many others
have dealt with similar issues.

your pain may seem insurmountable,
yet, you learn how others have dealt with theirs.

we are part of a human collective.
we are part of a whole.
when one of us goes through something,
someone else is out there
who's gone through something similar.

everything shall pass.
someone is out there to help you
and to love you.
open up to the love that is out there.
open up to time's ability to heal.

healing and loving
are natural.

holding onto pain and suffering
is not natural.
it is up to you to choose.

06

bursting through

i want to burst through the fear,
and be known for my courage.

bursting through the fear
is a daily decision
that i continually choose to make.

i want to shed the insecurities
that bind me.
i want to stop
over-protecting myself.
i want to truly live.
i want to burst through
any cage that i put myself in.

07

be that girl

be that girl
that you know you are.
she's waiting for you
to unleash her.
she's not afraid of success
because she knows
that she is worthy of it.
she's ready to face life's challenges
understanding that the only thing
she can control
is her attitude.

be that girl.
the girl who stands up
for herself
in the face of adversity
and lets her voice be heard.
she's brave enough
to let others see her thrive,
yet humble enough
to share how she does it.

be that girl
that you know you are.

she's confident.

she's creative.

she's classy yet goofy.

she's a go-getter,

but can always take a break.

she's friendly and kind.

she's ferociously optimistic.

she's you.

08

decide

decide
and don't look back.

make that decision
with gumption.

be the version
of you that you want
to be.

when you're in the moment,
be the main character of your story.

choose you.
choose life.
then ride the wave!

09

the morning euphoria

what does your true self
want to do in the morning?
perhaps, you long to sing
like the birds
or stretch out like an animal
or even rest a bit longer like
a turtle retreating into its shell.

what would you do
if your mind
wasn't planning the future
or replaying the past?

breathe in
to be present.
try to let the mind play out
and then assign it to focus
on your breathing.

breathe in
to be present
again and again.
trust the process
of being in the moment.

10

fulfillment

the road map to fulfillment
lies deep within our mind.
each one of us has
a unique path
to discover this feeling.

the world tries to sell you
ways to fulfillment,
but this experience
does not abide by a formula.
it cannot be bought.

the road to fulfillment
asks that one share their heart.
this brave act opens up your ability
to receive the flow
of abundance from the universe.

having the courage to expose
a deep part of your soul
infuses your life.
this spark ignites
the framework for fulfillment.
it can be such a simple process

that emerges when you let your guard down.

do not hide what is inside of you.
share it.
celebrate it.
be it.

van ekeren

chapter seven

take the leap

01

take the leap

i find myself
at the edge,
yet again.
shall i take the leap,
or shall i retreat and stay safe?

i breathe in.
i am the main character
of this story, of my story.
i know what i want to do.
i know that i will take the leap.

the doubts are part of living.
they will always be here.
i live with them
and hold their hands.
we are one.

i take the leap.
i am going to choose to live.
i am going to allow the fear
to transform
into excitement.
this is it.

02

it's all about you

remember
that you're
the main character
of your story.

work on your relationship
with yourself first,
then everyone else.

this inner bond
will strengthen every other one.

when your inner world
is healthy,
you can help change
our world.

03

focused energy

this sounds like
intense work,
but focused energy
can be simple,
profound
and comfortable.

it takes
courage to admit
what one wants.
it takes
focused energy
to get it.

get off the treadmill
that the world put in front of you.
sit with your thoughts.
be in your mind.

what is it
that you actually want?
who do you
want to be?

allow the answers to emerge.

listen.

integrate your answers,

and then live them out

with joy.

04

keep evolving

keep evolving.
there's no wrong way
to be you.

keep letting life
change you.
don't hold back.
don't try to protect yourself
in extreme ways.
relax your shoulders.
you're going to be okay.
in fact,
you're going to soar.

enjoy the uneasy moments.
fall into the pain.
feel it.
don't run from it.
let it change you.
you're evolving.

life wants you to be flexible
and buoyant.
when you retreat into a shell,

you calcify.
learn from those that did this
and invite them out of their shell
when they're ready.

know who you are.
don't be scared to shine.
your only job
is to be you.
you don't have to save anyone.
let them do their work.

just
keep evolving.

05

it's okay to be completely happy

be brave.
be happy.
share your joy.
nothing is as scary
as your mind makes it.

smile.
let the worries go.
has worrying helped anyone?
i know you know all of this.
just remember,
it's okay to be completely happy.

06

setting a living intention

the art of
setting a living intention
involves how one performs
each and every daily act.

it means
living in this world
amongst all types of energy,
yet infusing your particular poetry into
everything that you do.

this is a living intention.
this is breathing into life.
this is poetry in motion.

07

the lighter side of life

life is as heavy or as light
as i make it.
my processing unit,
my mind,
is the determining factor.

i choose to see the sunny days
and to embolden others to do so.

i choose to live on the lighter side of it all.

will you meet me there?

08

you get to be you

oh, to fully grasp
the notion
of the gift we all possess
that we get to be who we are.

i could write and write about this gift,
and then totally forget
and need someone else
to remind me of it.

are we wired to forget
so we can connect with one another
on a level of vulnerability?
or so we can help one another
and by doing so
help ourselves?
or so we can continue
to pursue inner alignment?

either way,
the one answer we always know
is that we get to be
who we are.
let's focus on that.

09

today is a fresh start

regardless of
what happened yesterday,
you get to leave the past
behind you.
you get to dive
into the newness
of today's sunrise.

today is a fresh start.
it's a package called the present.
it's an opportunity
to see possibilities.

let the old worries go.
declare today
as the start
of fresh and healthy habits.

do not harbor resentment
over the past
or anyone
who's hurt you.
choose to love and forgive
for you.

holding anything against someone
blocks the flow of
healthy energy.

forgive to live
your best life.
forgive yourself.
forgive others.
see the possibilities
that this new day brings.
choose right action
and right thought.
choose you.

10

the intention of the action

as i shift my mind
to focus on
the intention of my action,
the outcome of my work
becomes more tangible,
more attainable,
more rewarding
and more definable
in my own unique terms.

i used to feel that i needed
to control the results,
the fruits of my labor,
rather than the labor itself.

it is
the work
that matters.

it is
the intention
that i put into my actions
that matters.

this is the shift
that will change my lens
and help me see myself more clearly.
this is the shift
that will help me
feel proud of my contributions.

i had been waiting
for a particular result
as a sign of success.

i can see now
that the desired outcome
truly lies in the intention of the action.
i get to act
in a focused manner
to reveal something within myself,
not necessarily the recipient
of my work or actions.

it is
the intention
behind the work
that matters.

11

trust

trust
is
letting the wind of life
take your sails.

self trust
is
maintaining those sails.

it's learning how
to see in the dark.

it's clicking into
intuition.

it's navigating on choppy waters
with hopes of smooth sailing.

it's a work in progress.
it's full of possiblities.

12

life shares itself with you

the sky surrenders its beauty
to anyone who is willing to look up.
the air delivers its oxygen
to our lungs as we breathe it in.
the water allows itself to be consumed
by all who drink it.
the earth shares its nourishment with us
allowing us to harvest it and then consume its
riches.

life shares every part of itself
with us.
how do we give back?
trust.

when life seems challenging
and shares something with you
that is painful,
surrender to it.
the essence of life
is far wiser than our minds
can comprehend.
breathe in
to feel the present moment.

rest into today,

for life is a miracle.

accept its gifts

with no judgement.

allow life to sculpt you.

trust its benevolent nature.

13

waking up on the right side of life

how we wake up
is up to us.
it's our time
to reconnect
and rejuvenate ourselves
from the inside out.

waking up
on the right side of life
is a daily decision.

it feels good
to rise up
with hope and joy
and enthusiasm.

it feels good
to be a cheerleader
for your own life.

take the wheel and steer.
choose how you feel
and wake up with excitement
for what lies ahead of you.

van ekeren

.

About the Author

Nikki Van Ekeren is a writer and an artist. Her style of poetry is rooted in optimism, self growth and an appreciation for nature.

She is fascinated with the process of inner discovery and learning how to empower oneself.

Her other poetry books include *Grace & Grit, These Poems Are About Sunny Days*, and for children, *You Get to Be You.*

Made in the USA
Monee, IL
16 June 2021

71435034R00075